AMAZING SCIENCE
ELECTRICITY

Sally Hewitt

WAYLAND

First published in Great Britain in 2006 by
Wayland, an imprint of Hachette Children's Books

This paperback edition published in 2008 by Wayland

Wayland, 338 Euston Road, London NW1 3BH

Copyright © 2006 Wayland

Senior Editor: Joyce Bentley
Senior Design Manager: Rosamund Saunders
Designer: Tall Tree

British Library Cataloguing in Publication Data
Hewitt, Sally,
       Electricity - (Amazing Science)
       1. Electricity - Juvenile Literature
       I. Title
       537

ISBN: 978-0-7502-5496-0

Printed and bound in China

Cover Lightning hitting Sugar Loaf Mountain, Rio de Janeiro
Title page: girl with static electric hair

Nasa 6, Jim Craigmyle/Corbis 7, Getty Images 8, Roy
McMahon/Corbis 9, Chris Mellor/Getty Images 10, Lester
Lefkowitz/Getty images 11, Fernand Ivaldi/Getty Images 12,
Rick Gomez/Corbis 13, George Grall/ Getty Images 14,
Helene Rogers/Art Directors 15, Alison Wright/Corbis 16,
Roger Ressmeyer/Corbis 17, Louis K. Melsel Gallery,
Inc./Corbis 18, Thomas Hoeffgen/Getty images 19, Pascal Le
Segretain/Getty Images 20, Helene Rogers/Art Directors 21,
Philip Wilkins 22-23, Henning von Hollenben/Getty Images
24, Jeremy Liebman/Getty Images 25, Peter Hendrie/Getty
Images 26, Royalty-Free/Corbis 27.

Wayland is a division of Hachette Children's Books,
an Hachette Livre UK Company

Contents

Amazing electricity

Electricity is very powerful. It lights up big cities so brightly you can see them shining from space.

Electricity is a kind of energy. Electricity gives lights energy to shine.

It gives machines the energy to work and electric heaters the energy to give out heat.

YOUR TURN!

Find machines at home that use electricity to work.

A computer needs electricity to work but pens do not.

Natural electricity

Lightning is natural electricity. You see it as a huge spark flashing between storm clouds and the ground.

Lightning is a kind of static electricity.

When you rub a balloon against your hair, you make static electricity.

Static electricity makes the balloon pull your hair towards it.

YOUR TURN!

Rub a balloon on a woollen sleeve. Now watch static electricity make the balloon stick to the wall.

SCIENCE WORDS: **lightning   natural   static**

Making electricity

Electricity is made in giant power stations. Oil, gas or coal is burned to heat water into steam.

Energy from the steam is turned into electricity.

We also use energy from the sun, the wind and moving water to make electricity.

YOUR TURN!

Why won't energy from the sun, wind and water run out?

No oil, gas or coal is burned to make electricity from these wind turbines.

SCIENCE WORDS: power station   turbine

11

Using electricity

Electricity makes machines work.
It makes lights flash, escalators
move and music play.

Electricity flows from power stations along cables. It comes into buildings through a socket in the wall.

To make a machine work you have to plug it in and switch it on.

YOUR TURN!

What would stop working at home if the electricity was turned off?

▲ Electricity flows along a wire into a hairdryer.

SCIENCE WORDS: cable flow

13

Danger!

An electric eel uses electricity as a weapon. It can kill another animal for food with an electric shock.

Electricity can be dangerous. A strong electric shock could kill you.

Electricity flows through water. Turning on a switch with wet hands could give you a shock.

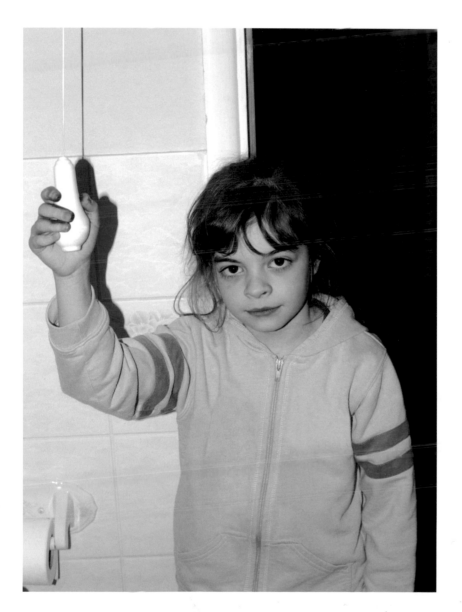

A bathroom's light switch is turned on using a cord. It will stop you getting a shock.

YOUR TURN!

Always use electricity safely. Don't touch anything electric with wet hands. Never put fingers in sockets.

SCIENCE WORDS: dangerous   shock

Moving along

An electric train speeds along a track.
An electric rail on the ground
gives it the power to move.

An electric train has a big motor that uses a lot of electricity.

A toy train has a small motor that uses a little electricity.

Electricity runs through the tracks into the toy train.

YOUR TURN!

Find things at home that need electricity to move. Do they move along, to and fro or round and round?

SCIENCE WORDS: motor rail

Batteries

These robots light up, talk and move. All they need to give them energy are small batteries.

Batteries are power packs for small machines that don't use much electricity.

The battery makes electricity when the machine is turned on.

 A battery gives a torch the power to shine.

YOUR TURN!

Find things that use batteries to work.

SCIENCE WORDS: battery robot

On and off

Turning on one switch can light up thousands of coloured lights. All the lights are joined by electric wires.

When you turn on a light switch, electricity flows along wires and lights up the bulb.

When you turn the switch off, electricity stops flowing and the light goes out.

A switch joins and breaks an electric circuit to turn electricity on and off.

YOUR TURN!

Find electric switches in the wall and on machines. Just look, don't touch!

SCIENCE WORDS: switch   wire   join

Make a circuit

Electricity flows round and round in a circle or circuit. Ask an adult to help you make a simple circuit.

You need a bulb, a bulb holder, two wires with clips and a battery pack.

Join one end of each wire to the battery pack. Join the other ends to the bulb holder.

YOUR TURN!

Can you explain why the light goes out when the circuit is broken?

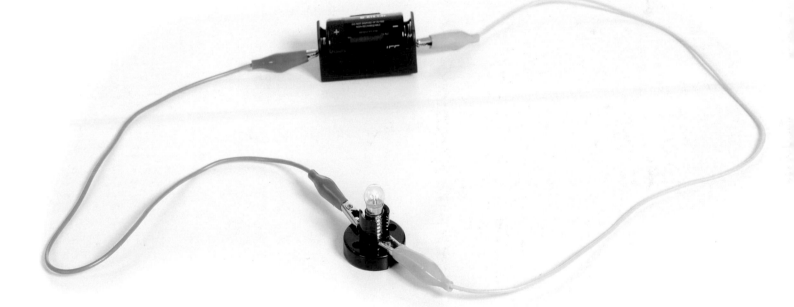

The light shines when the circuit is joined. It goes out if you break the circuit.

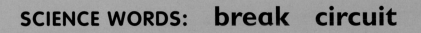

SCIENCE WORDS: **break   circuit**

23

Life without electricity

When you camp in a field of a campsite you can light fires for cooking and keeping warm.

Electricity was first used in homes about **100** years ago.

Before electricity, people lit fires for cooking and washed and cleaned by hand.

YOUR TURN!

Do you think washing, rinsing and wringing out your school shirt is hard work? Try it and see!

Washing clothes by hand can be hard work.

SCIENCE WORDS: **fire   hard work**

Save electricity

Burning oil, gas and coal to make electricity fills the air with dirty smoke. One day these fuels will run out.

We waste a lot of electricity at home and at school every day.

Saving electricity helps to keep the air cleaner and saves oil, gas and coal.

Shut doors and windows to keep the heat in.

SCIENCE WORDS: fuels save waste

27

Glossary

Battery
A power pack that makes electricity. Batteries give things such as torches, radios and clocks the power to work.

Break
When something breaks it comes apart in pieces. When an electric circuit breaks, the wires come apart and electricity can't flow round it.

Cable
A thick wire. Electricity flows along cables from power stations into our homes.

Circuit
A circuit is a loop or a circle. Electricity flows round and round in a circuit.

Dangerous
Something that is dangerous can hurt you. Electricity can be dangerous if you don't use it safely.

Electricity
A kind of energy that we use to give things the power to work.

Energy
Energy such as electrcity, coal or food is burned to give things and people the power to work.

Fire
A fire burns and gives out heat and light.

Flow
A way of moving along. Water flows out of a tap. Electricity flows along wires.

Fuels
A material from the ground that is made into energy such as oil, gas or coal.

Hard work
Work is a job that has to be done. You use a lot of energy to do hard work.

Join
When things are joined, they are put together.

Lightning
A kind of natural electricity we see as a flash in the sky and hear as thunder.

Motor
A machine that makes things move.

Natural
Natural things haven't been made by hand or in a factory.

Power station
A place where electricity is made.

Power
The force that makes things move and work.

Rail
Trains move along metal rails called railway tracks.

Robot
A machine that can move, light up, make noises and get work done.

Save
When you save something, you don't waste it.
You only use as much as you need.

Shock
A sudden blow. A strong electric shock can kill you.

Static
If something is static it doesn't move. Static electricity stays in one place.

Switch
A switch turns things on and off

Turbine
A machine with blades that spin very fast to make electricity.

Waste
When we waste something, we use more than we need.

Wire
A long, thin piece of metal. Electricity flows along electric wires.

Index